TULLY MONSTER
A First Look

HANNAH GRAMSON

Lerner Publications ◆ Minneapolis

Educator Toolbox

Reading books is a great way for kids to express what they're interested in. Before reading this title, ask the reader these questions:

- What do you think this book is about? Look at the cover for clues.
- What do you already know about Tully monsters?
- What do you want to learn about Tully monsters?

Let's Read Together

Encourage the reader to use the pictures to understand the text.

Point out when the reader successfully sounds out a word.

Praise the reader for recognizing sight words such as *the* and *and*.

TABLE OF CONTENTS

Tully Monsters 4

You Connect! 21
STEM Snapshot 22
Photo Glossary 23
Learn More 23
Index 24

Tully Monsters

Tully monsters were fish. They lived three hundred million years ago.

Tully monsters lived in the ocean.

What other animals live in the ocean?

Tully monsters were small. The biggest were only 14 inches (36 cm) long.

That is about the size of a shoebox.

They had two eyes.

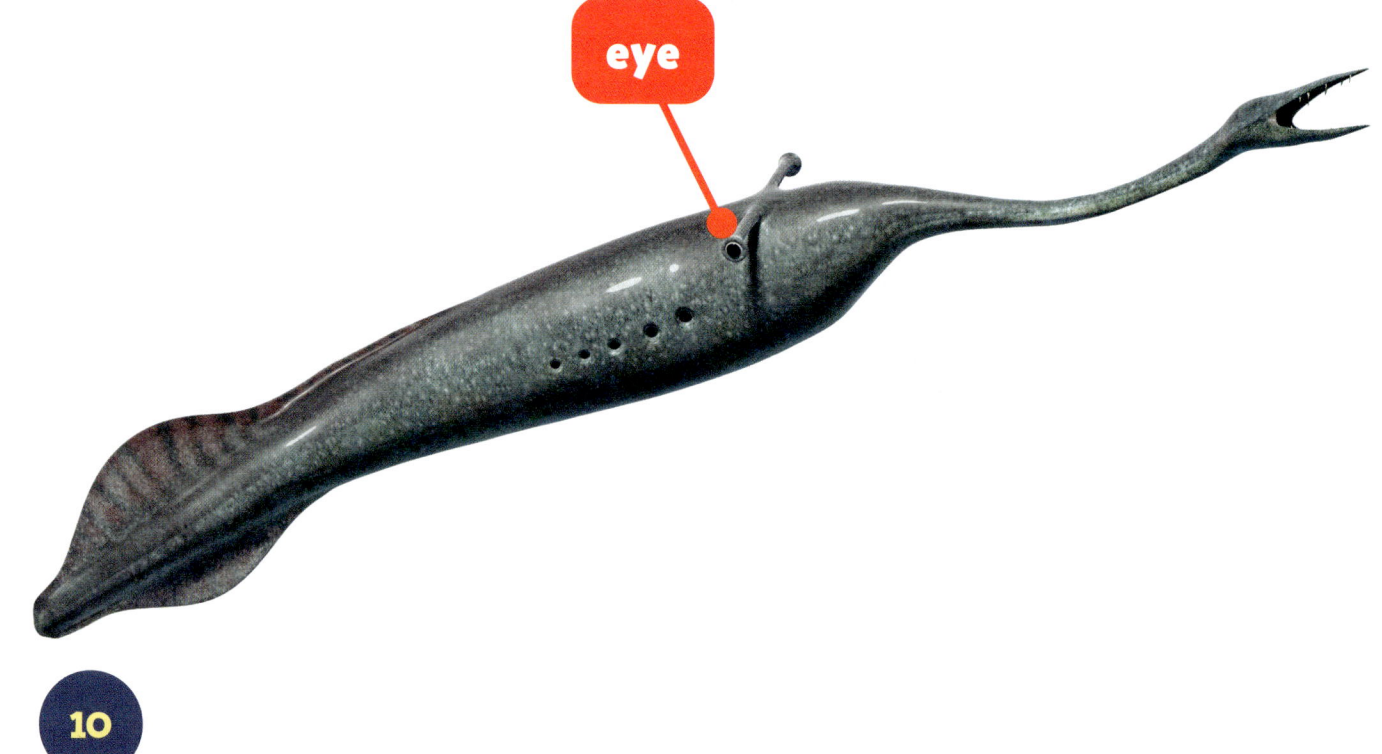

eye stalk

The eyes were on stalks like a snail's eyes.

They had long trunks.

What other animals have long trunks?

How might sharp teeth be helpful?

Their trunks had a claw at the end. The claw had sharp teeth.

They used their claw to grab food as crabs do.

They may have eaten plants and small sea animals.

People learned about Tully monsters from their fossils.

You Connect!

What do you like about Tully monsters?

Would you want to meet a Tully monster?

What other sea animals would you like to learn about?

STEM Snapshot

Encourage students to think and ask questions as scientists do. Ask the reader:

What have you learned about Tully monsters?

What have you noticed about the way Tully monsters looked?

What do you still want to learn about Tully monsters?

Photo Glossary

Learn More

Gramson, Hannah. *Megalodon: A First Look*. Minneapolis: Lerner Publications, 2026.

Gregory, Josh. *Discover the Ichthyosaurus*. Ann Arbor, MI: Cherry Lake, 2025.

Murray, Julie. *Mosasaurus*. Minneapolis: Dash! Leveled Readers, 2025.

Index

claw, 15–16
fossils, 20
ocean, 6–7
stalks, 11
trunk, 12–13, 15

Photo Acknowledgments

Jose Antonio Penas/Science Source, p. 5; Georgette Douwma/Getty Images, p. 7; Dotted Yeti/Shutterstock, pp. 8, 10, 14, 23; Vladimir Sukhachev/Getty Images, p. 9; DaveAlan/Getty Images, pp. 11, 23; dottedhippo/Getty Images, p. 13 (top); Vicki Jauron, Babylon and Beyond Photography, pp. 13 (bottom), 23; James Kuether/Science Source, p. 17 (top); Natalia Harper/Alamy, p. 17 (bottom); Vincent Pommeyrol/Getty Images, p. 19; Mark Lopez/Argonne National Laboratory/US Department of Energy, pp. 20, 23.
Cover image: Nobumichi Tamura/Stocktrek Images/Getty Images.

Copyright © 2026 by Lerner Publishing Group, Inc.

All rights reserved. International copyright secured. No part of this book may be reproduced, stored in a retrieval system, or transmitted in any form or by any means—electronic, mechanical, photocopying, recording, or otherwise—without the prior written permission of Lerner Publishing Group, Inc., except for the inclusion of brief quotations in an acknowledged review.

Lerner Publications Company
An imprint of Lerner Publishing Group, Inc.
241 First Avenue North
Minneapolis, MN 55401 USA

For reading levels and more information, look up this title at www.lernerbooks.com.

Main body text set in Mikado Medium.
Typeface provided by Hannes von Doehren.

Editor: Annie Zheng
Photo Editor: Cynthia Zemlicka

Library of Congress Cataloging-in-Publication Data

Names: Gramson, Hannah, author.
Title: Tully monster : a first look / Hannah Gramson.
Description: Minneapolis, MN, USA : Lerner Publications, [2026] | Series: Read about prehistoric beasts (read for a better world) | Includes bibliographical references and index. | Audience term: Children | Audience: Ages 5-8 | Audience: Grades K-1 | Summary: "Tully monsters lived in Earth's oceans about 300 million years ago. From how they might have eaten to how they looked, readers will discover interesting facts about this prehistoric sea creature"— Provided by publisher.
Identifiers: LCCN 2024055129 (print) | LCCN 2024055130 (ebook) | ISBN 9798765669099 (lib. bdg.) | ISBN 9798765684733 (pbk.) | ISBN 9798765680537 (epub)
Subjects: LCSH: Tullimonstrum gregarium—Juvenile literature. | Tullimonstrum—Juvenile literature.
Classification: LCC QE766 .G73 2026 (print) | LCC QE766 (ebook) | DDC 560—dc23/eng/20241226

LC record available at https://lccn.loc.gov/2024055129
LC ebook record available at https://lccn.loc.gov/2024055130

Manufactured in the United States of America
1-1011836-53880-2/25/2025